David
Bowie

Out of the Cool

DAVID BOWIE

Out of the Cool

Photographs by Philip Kamin

Text by Peter Goddard

Beaufort Books

New York   Toronto

Library of Congress Cataloging in Publication Data
Goddard, Peter.
David Bowie, out of the cool.
1. Bowie, David. 2. Rock musicians — England —
Biography. I. Kamin, Philip. II. Title.
ML420.B7782G6 1983   784.5′4′00924 [B] 83-11916

ISBN 0-8253-0181-5

Published in the United States by
Beaufort Books
9 East 40th Street
New York, New York
10016

First Edition

10 9 8 7 6 5 4 3 2 1

Printed and bound in Canada

Book design by **Joe Stevens Graphic Design**

Address correspondence to Philip Kamin and
Peter Goddard, P.O. Box 1501, 5647 Yonge Street,
Willowdale, Ontario, Canada M2M 3T2

Acknowledgments

For Bill

I would especially like to thank Peter Goddard, Alan Edwards, Steve Mandel, the Borneo Horns, and the entire David Bowie organization.

Very special thanks to Brad Simon, my assistant in the United States and Canada, and to Cathy Spanton for travel arrangements. Special mention for Robert Bonneville, Linda Shields, Brian Kirsh, and Rama Bhat.

I would also like to thank Allan Stokell, Don Hood and C. J. Morgan at Positive Images, Toronto; Doug Paddey, Marty Ingles and Gary Beck at Canon Cameras of Canada; Steve Coomber at Ilford Films; Bob, Glen and Skip at Steichenlab, Toronto.

P.K.

Thanks to Don for his patience, to my womenfolk, for theirs ... and to Philip.

P.G.

Photographs of DAVID BOWIE and the SERIOUS MOONLIGHT TOUR were taken in Europe, England, Canada, and the United States.

WHEREIN WE MEET OUR HERO AND HEAR OF HIS PLAN
— LET'S DANCE — SAYING A SERIOUS
GOODBYE TO ZIGGY.

The black Mercedes slices around the corner, parting and scattering tourists before it makes a high-and-tight wheels-squealing U-turn and slams to a dead stop in front of the Brussels Sheraton.

Sweet holy geez, Edna — what's this?

The clump of plump American businessmen and their wives jumps out of the way even before the doors open. They back up into the crazy lady and her even crazier dog — a pair who have been waiting outside the hotel day and night now. The couples freeze in their tracks.

The German shepherd's muzzle is frozen in a vicious snarl. The owner is snarling too. Both of them have come to feel mean and tired...

But what do six middle-aged citizens of the great American Midwest care about snarling Belgian crazies? Do they notice that the dog's hair is dyed or there's this crazy Z painted down across its nose?

Do they notice the owner's own orange hair? Humph. They don't even see the two kids on scooters who've been chasing the Mercedes. The kids almost crash into one another. Instead, they crash into the curb. And the Americans don't see anything — except *him*.

Rushing out of the Mercedes and into the perpetual golden beige twilight of the hotel lobby is David Bowie.

But it's not Bowie himself who has them dazzled — not the fact of who he is. (In fact, as I watch them it's apparent they're not sure *who* he is.)

It's the look on his face, a strange exalted look. He appears to be exhausted and paler than pale. He's sweating.

The sweet little brush of blond hair, so artfully casual in his publicity shots, is swept back now, and the gazers can see the sheer tension strung like telephone lines across his forehead.

And in an instant the Americans understand *exactly* what they've seen. Victory. It's dazzling. It's even frightening in its way. It's what they've seen on the faces of American presidents after winning re-election to a second term, or on boxers' after going twelve rounds with an opponent they really feared.

It's *triumph*.

The first date of his first tour in five years is just finished and Bowie knows it's going to work. The whole thing is going to work. He doesn't need to wait for the rest of Europe, or the North American, Japanese, or Australian portions of the tour, where it will all come to an end in the winter. He doesn't need to wonder what a concert movie might look like. He doesn't need to worry about criticism good or bad. It works. The plan works.

The blond man vanishes into the beige, the couples head out into the night for the excitement they'll never find, and the crazies clump away, snarling at each other.

"But he knew he'd have to give away something of himself. He couldn't afford to be so remote or cool."

The word spread through all the media, before the tour, was that he'd relaxed. He was, it was pointed out, closer to forty years old than thirty. He was a single parent. He'd mellowed.

Far from it. If anything, Bowie's sense of purpose was never greater. After all the early failures and all the years of waiting and wondering, he sensed it was his turn, now. "But he knew he'd have to give away something of himself," one friend said. "He couldn't afford to be so remote or cool."

So the plan became a strategy of emotions. He would be the man who came in from the cool. But this would involve artistic tactics as well — meeting with Nile Rogers at Bemelman's Bar in the Carlisle Hotel to discuss the possibility of Rodgers producing a new accessible Bowie album, and eventually phoning Carlos Alomar, his long-time concert master and arranger, to put together a touring band.

"All of the attention has been nice, but the tour was planned long before that came along," Bowie told me just after the *Let's Dance* album was out, co-produced by Bowie and Rodgers. "I just felt it was time I did something."

This is where Nile Rodgers comes in. A sophisticated New Yorker whose feel for music goes back much further than his years (his thirtieth birthday coincided with the tour), he was approached the fall before by Bowie.

Rodgers and partner, Bernard Edwards, had a hit with Chic, their own group, then with Sister Sledge (*We Are Family*) and Diana Ross (*Upside Down*, which he wrote) and Deborah Harry. But the pair had decided to launch their own solo efforts when Rodgers first bumped into Bowie.

Nothing came of it until one afternoon in October — "it was not quite cold yet" — and Rodgers was at his home in Connecticut because some workmen were fixing his place.

Rodgers: "So one of the guys — they were all from New Jersey and had real New Jersey accents — came out and said, 'Hey, Nile, there's a David Bowie on the line.' I thought he was joking, but the guy said, 'Hey Nile, no, it's really David Bowie.'

"So we set up a meeting at Bemelman's Bar at the Carlisle Hotel and we must have sat next to each other for twenty minutes without realizing it. He didn't recognize me and I didn't recognize him. We both went out and phoned our road managers before we finally got together.

"Here I was expecting someone with red hair, you know, Ziggy Stardust or something, and here was this...average-looking guy. I'd always admired his stuff but I'd always seen him as eclectic and artsy.

"That's not what he wanted, though. He did all the writing and I did all the arrangements and along the way he taught me a valuable lesson — that you can be musically accessible and still be yourself.

"He had his own definite concept about what he wanted from the *Let's Dance* album and from his music at this time. But whatever else it was, it stayed David Bowie music.

"What I've always liked doing with my music — and it's true about his music as well — is to write on several levels at once. You should never give a clear message. You should shroud it in some way. This way you give the listener something to discover. With Chic, we wrote *Good Times* right at the heart of the recession. With Bowie, there was always a double message."

Brussels — the largest city in Belgium — is also by some accounts the quietest. Some would even say the dullest. The *Mannekin-Pis*, a bronze statue of a boy urinating, dating from 1619, is its best-known landmark. It's about as racy as things get. The porn flicks you can catch in neat little movie houses off the old Grand' Place are heavily

censored. It is as tension-free as a city can get these days.

For most of its early history, Brussels was a market town free from the vicious whims of any single ruler. Still without any particular brand of paranoia or chic new urban fear, it remains devoted to its calm orderly method of doing business, and everyone who lives there seems to like it that way.

So does David Bowie. Frankfurt was slated to be the official opening of the Serious Moonlight Tour, and for good reason: Frankfurt would bring him back to Germany and kicking off the tour there would become a spiritual home-coming of sorts after all those years he spent in Germany in the late '70s.

In theory, then, Brussels was only a warm-up. Yet that's not the way it appeared — there was nothing about the two shows in the Voorst National to convince the 6,000 or so kids packed in each night that they were anything less than solid. The tour had in fact officially begun.

What a coup this proved to be, though, — for Bowie to pull off the equivalent of a Broadway opening in New York in the one city which would not allow itself to be dragged into any star-tripping. Better, to begin *the media event of the year* *without most of the media*.

The Stones began the '81 tour in a massive, public fashion, before huge crowds in Philadelphia's John F. Kennedy Stadium. In '83 The Who launched the beginning of their end in Washington and were immediately media-ized.

For Bowie, much of the British and European press showed up in Frankfurt two nights after he'd opened in Brussels. And he was ready for them. His show was honed.

The media folks were fretting about getting press passes in the lobby of the towering Frankfurt Plaza hotel long after Carlos Alomar knew that the crucial transition from *Fashion* to *Let's Dance* worked perfectly.

That is the way Bowie has come to like it — always slightly ahead with the press always catching up. But make no mistake about it: he makes sure the press does catch up.

Years ago there was a single all-embracing theory about Bowie's career. It went like this—that he only came into his own when he stopped trying to be the next great all-round music hall star and plunged head-long into rock.

The Voorst National is a squat, nondescript hall on the edge between the city and the suburbs. Like the hall, the crowds are cozy; there are no hassles, no pushing, no screaming or yelling.

Where are the original Bowie freaks? There are no mini-Ziggy Stardusts. No Thin White Dukes. These are just kids mostly, school kids, very ragtag and crumpled in their old T-shirts, baggy pants, knitted sweaters and scarves. Loose and happy, the kids have come to love to dance down that stairway the bass line in *Let's Dance* takes you down.

Eventually, all the scruff and casualness would cause one British critic to sniff, "There are no more than sixty or seventy acceptably dressed people in the entire audience." For me, though, the lack of tension was heaven.

We'd been warned early on that no cameras would be allowed, that anyone even suspected of carrying any sort of photographic device would be frisked and searched. As it turned out, every sort of device short of a television Port-A-Pac unit made its way in. Still no hassles.

We're packed down and down into the bowl-shaped hall with everyone jostling everyone else. Then I notice something. No one's talking about Bowie. No one's anticipating what might happen. None of his old pop-mythical baggage is brought out to be rummaged through. This was a crowd that didn't appear to care.

But a bit of history here. Years ago there was a single all-embracing theory about Bowie's career. It went like this — that he only came into his own when he stopped trying to be the next great all-round music hall star and plunged head-long into rock.

Anthony Newley was the role model at the start. At least, that's what Bowie's first manager, Ken Pitt, had had in mind for him. That strategy was revamped soon enough. Pitt was out and Tony DeFries was in. And along with the arrival of DeFries, the show business lawyer from Shepherd's Bush, came Bowie's Ziggy Stardust persona.

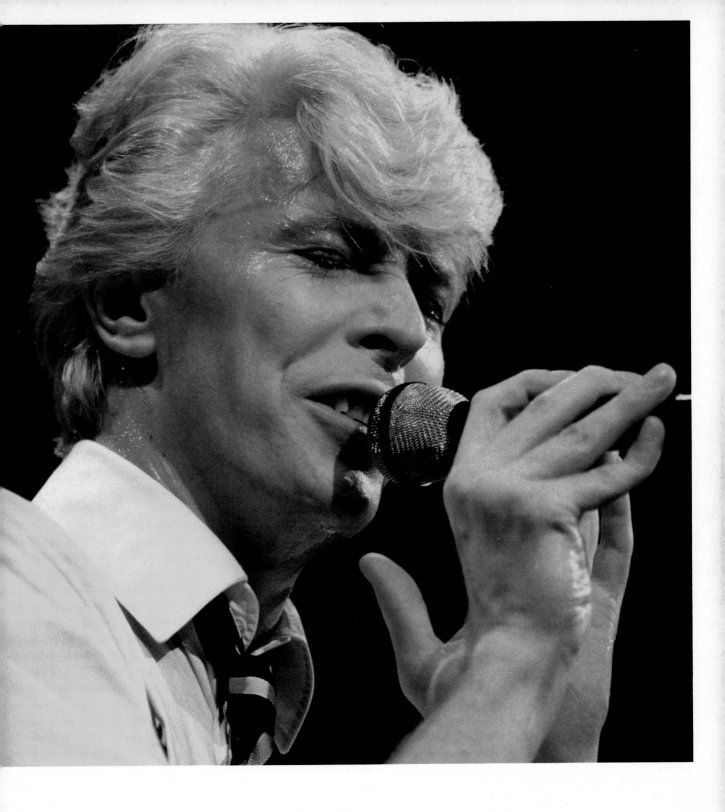

The idea of the all-round entertainer was jettisoned for that of the idea of the star. The capital-S Star — the larger-than-life figure who would come to exist only in one time, place, and style. Bowie was still Bowie without Ziggy. With Ziggy he was a hit.

At least that's been one view of how his career has worked out. But one look at the stage of the Serious Moonlight Tour, and at the pale creamy beige suit he wears, tells you that the theory is incomplete. Bowie may have ditched Ziggy, but he's forgotten none of Pitt's lessons. This is good old-fashioned show-biz, the kind Anthony Newley would recognize instantly.

Serious Moonlight indeed. The stage is stark. There's a ruined city look about it. Dull grey images of ancient columns in decay are to either side. A worn and pitted beam runs parallel to the stage across the stop. At the very back tower huge plastic containers, shimmering and pale.

Very cool all of this, and passionate and sexy. For all his intellectualism, sex has always been a subtext of any David Bowie show. In the Diamond Dogs Tour of the late '70s, there was a rocket launcher on stage shaped like a penis — spurting blood yet. Metaphors continue apace. These plastic containers look like huge condoms. To stage right a huge ashen grey hand points into the sky: on stage left there's a pale, crescent moon.

"That's what the song is about," I remember him saying about *Let's Dance* from where the line "under the serious moonlight" comes. "It was to make something that sounded like disco but had the feeling that it was the *last* dance."

At the press conference in London in the spring of '83, when he announced the tour, he promised simplicity and directness. What he didn't explain, however, was just how complex an idea this would be.

Lindsay Kemp, the British mime, teacher, and blithe spirit, took Bowie into his troupe when Bowie's career was at its lowest ebb. Late in 1967 the singer went out on tour with the mime, an unpaid and generally unnoticed member of the troupe.

For all that's changed in Bowie's life, those few months with Kemp have not been forgotten. Kemp talks about being "only interested in passionate theater." Bowie's show is just that — rich, romantic, and terribly passionate.

But the teaching went further. Kemp passed on to his pupil some ideas of how to make the most impact out of the least movement: "the importance of stillness on stage."

Bowie makes stillness an active ingredient. The rigidity of his body — the tightness in his back, the tension around his mouth — becomes its own kind of theater.

So there he is, out on stage, and the act's begun even before you realize. It's all done simply and effortlessly. Quickly enough, the set itself is forgotten. The band, complete with horn section and two singers in striped blazers, rings the stage behind him. They're like characters marooned in some designer's version of a Micronesian island. It looks a bit like a store-window display. Carlos Alomar is in an Indian Sherwani, looking with his enormous glasses like a Indian provincial academic; Carmine Rojas, the bassist who once backed Stevie Wonder, would seem to be from Madagascar. Earl Slick, the guitarist brought in at the last moment to replace

Stevie Ray Vaughan, is another exotic — the '60s hippy, complete with headband.

Taken together with the Borneo Horns, as the horn section has come to call itself, everyone is equally exotic, and they only further emphasize Bowie's *whiteness*.

And the more they move, the more they emphasize how deliberate he is about everything.

Mind you, it's not that he isn't moving. He grabs the mike with his left hand and leans back from the waist for *Rock And Roll With Me*. His hands move. His right hand darts out before his eyes and he cuts the air in a face-level jab.

But every motion is compact and crisp. His self-control is awesome. The lighting is gentle and unobtrusive; the stage is lush with pastel colors. Rather than seeming soft or, at the other extreme, giving all, you can sense his steely discipline.

If he does nothing else, he'll have changed the whole notion of lighting the rock'n'roll stage. He used static and brilliant white light for his Station To Station Tour — an idea which likely reflected his attempts at the time to bring discipline to his life. But nothing in that dazzling, obsessively white stage can match all the pastel power here.

We were told by the booming voice of an anonymous announcer that the show would be in two parts. The first segment seems like a warm-up though. It runs smoothly and almost too orderly. Bowie's on automatic. But then there's one small curve in the straight and narrow road when he sings "Lavender Blue, dilly, dilly..." in his most confident, cabaret voice. It's a lead-in to *Heroes*.

We don't know — at least at this point — that it's all a set-up for the rest of the show: that the lull is deliberate and designed to highlight what will be a run-away finale.

What In The World and *Joe The Lion* follow, then there's *Wild Is The Wind*. It's all pure British music hall and more proof than anyone needs that the Anthony Newley connection continues.

Bowie, friends will tell you, never really minded the idea of becoming the Euro-popstar of the '60s. One act he concocted early on was part-Dylan and part-cabaret schtick — Bowie as the British Charles Aznavour.

This year's show, as it was coming more and more apparent in the growing heat in the Voorst National, was cabaret on a grand scale. More specifically, it was a staged and designed as television version of cabaret. At the press conference in London in the spring of '83, when he announced the tour, he promised simplicity and directness. What he didn't explain, however, was just how complex an idea this would be.

As the band launches into *Golden Years*, they gather around Bowie who's sitting in a chair. They're looking — and in some cases pointing — off into the hall. The Sims brothers, Frank and George, the two multi-purpose singers on the tour, are in their striped jacket gamblers' gear. Far back on the stage is

Tony Thompson, the drummer, in the shadows. The lights dim to a golden bronze.

As with most songs, the orchestration has been changed sufficiently to bring a new mood and attitude to the piece. The core of what it's about remains the same, however. This *Golden Years* is reflective and the vocal harmonies are more pronounced.

He's up again. It's for *Fashion*. At first, the song seems matched, musically and emotionally, with *Golden Years*, the song it follows. What it turns out to be — and the entire show hinges on the fact — is an introduction to *Let's Dance*.

Some modest pantomime evolves from *Fashion* — suddenly he jogs back from the microphone, his arms tight to his sides, his hands balled into fists. He's boxing. He's also recreating the cover photo of his *Let's Dance* album.

And it's here where the show goes into overdrive.

Inside the hall there's only one enormous sound which matters — the hard-edged thump of the bass as its notes climb down the ostinato pattern for *Let's Dance*. On record the piece has always sounded somewhat frail — Nile Rodgers, you think, has made another thinking man's dance record. Live, it's something else again.

This bass line is awesome. It *is* the piece.

The crackling rhythm guitar counter-point is a minor distraction. Bowie's voice is curled up inside this bass line and it comes close to being lost completely.

The band shouts, "Let's Dance." It's where the show begins — and in a way it's where the tour begins as well. It puts this David Bowie retrospective into a completely modern framework. It also manages to strip away

layers of the old mythology from the pieces which follow: *Life On Mars, Sorrow, Cat People, China Girl* (where again the bass drives everything), *Scary Monsters* and *Rebel Rebel*. All are heard in the context of the cool raw modern power of *Let's Dance* — even *Rebel Rebel* is done as straight old rock'n'roll and allows us all to stomp right along.

The first half ends curiously. It's as if he's paying homage to his friends or influences — or both. First, there's *I Can't Explain*, a deliberate re-working of the old Who standard. Finally, there's the Velvet Underground's *White Light, White Heat*, a breakneck show-stopper which becomes a huge hit within the band itself.

It's his return to the "rock stage",
as the announcer here says.
Yet it's not the same stage,
the same rock'n'roll, or the same
Bowie, as he's letting us know.

Backstage, the pre-show tension is beginning to ease. Alomar had been worried that they didn't have enough time in Texas for rehearsals. Now it seems they did. (Throughout the tour, whatever the reviewers wrote about Bowie, the show or the tour, there was universal agreement that the band was first-rate.) When Earl Slick had to be brought in at the last moment, the planning seemed even shakier. But here, too, things worked out. Slick, the veteran Bowie sideman, caught up quickly with the rest.

There's a change of costume for the second half. Bowie is wearing a pale green suit cut almost identically (short in the sleeves, pants baggy) to the one for the first act. But there are slight differences — interesting differences. This pale green number has a crest stitched on it over the heart: a slim crescent moon floats on a deep blue background. There's something very European in all of this and something that hints of the private club.

The second half begins at a much higher

pitch than did the first. It's also without the subtleties — well, with one or two exceptions. Bowie holds the skull in front of him during *Cracked Actor* and I remember all the costumes, theatrics and lights — all that overblown drama, in short — which in the past used to go into this little bit of rock'n'roll Hamletry.

What this is I decide — what much of the entire night has been in fact — is a re-staging of past tours and past shows. The essence of the original scenes has been kept intact.

Then there's a break. And suddenly he starts to speak and the hall goes strangely silent. It's a curiously formal little speech, almost as if it had been prepared, written perhaps:

"I don't know how much of this is perspiration and how much is tears of happiness, but I can tell you I'm very happy to be here."

He's cheered but the cheering is hesitant. What he's just said has not revealed much.

Indeed, it reveals nothing. Instead, it has established an even more formal relationship between singer and audience. The almost antiquated flavor of the words is more reminiscent of what one of the Royal Family might say as she or he passes through some strange exotic outpost like Saskatoon or Canberra.

It's his return to the "rock stage," as the announcer here says. Yet it's not the same stage, the same rock'n'roll, or the same Bowie, as he's letting us know.

From *Ashes To Ashes* to *Young Americans* to *Fame*, the show takes on a panoramic quality as it comes to a close. Bowie on stately parade.

The hotel's quiet that night. The parties are all quiet too. A wayward photographer happens to walk through a door that's open to find the Borneo Horns quietly cheering

what they anticipate will come. They're not on this tour for the big bucks, they're on it for the exposure.

And how.

Could he have a couple of tickets for the second show in Brussels?, the photographer asks.

The horns debate the matter. One of them phones the photographer's room a little later. Yeah, he could have a couple of tickets.

"But please don't say where they've come from," says the particular horn on the line.

It was when his ego took all the battering it would take that he retreated behind the characters he'd dreamed up.

David Bowie's story is not as modern as we would have it. Nor is it as full of Edwardian decadence as some around him might have it. Rather, there is something distinctly Victorian about it. It is the story of the little boy who grew up poorly but ended up happy after a life of adventures and mishaps. It is in its way a modern *David Copperfield*.

But for *our* David, history was a triumph of the ego, not one over class.

His struggle has little to do with growing up poorly during unsettled times, although that played a small part. Rather it has to do with a sense of self. He was born David Robert Jones, January 8, 1947, in Brixton.

His step-brother Terry (from his mother's earlier marriage) was seven. It was Terry who was first interested in music, particularly the kind of cool, late-'40s early-'50s jazz that Bowie would eventually return to. The two would drift apart and Terry would end up in psychiatric care. (During the tour there'd be complaints that David was not doing enough for Terry.)

Right from the start, Bowie ran into resistance and hassles, roadblocks and out-and-out failure. There were also some oddities — a teenage punch-up over a girl resulted in paralysis in his left eye. There he was, a jazz freak, playing sax and all and along comes pop to make jazz unfashionable. None of his early bands — The King Bees, then Davy Jones & The Manish Boys then Davy Jones

& The Lower Third — were given much chance of success.

But ego comes in here — enough of ego to carry him through being dumped by one record company after another then having to drop his own name where there appeared another Davy Jones, one in the Monkees, yet.

It was when his ego took all the battering it would take that he retreated behind the characters he'd dreamed up. Through Lindsay Kemp he found how these characters moved: through a passing involvement with Buddhism he learned the distances into himself he can go to.

He was with Deram records, the burgeoning little company that also had signed Cat Stevens, when manager Ken Pitt made a

video to hustle some of his songs. Eventually Deram didn't want David Bowie on its label.

Casting about for what to do next, Pitt looked at the video again. And there, in a song, he found he was watching a strange new character...a space oddity.

He began to shape things after that. And if there is a point to the shape of his career, it's this — that it began as a vision where music was only a backdrop.

When Bowie arrived in Berlin that bleak year of his life, he found a colony of artists and musicians, a colony which ranged from Chris Burden to Iggy Pop, which was expanding the boundaries of what art could be.

Brian Eno's ambient music — for airports or elevators or whatever — was music that blurred the distinctions between the art event and the world around it. Iggy Pop brought shock tactics to his performances. Kraftwerk, like the Futurists of the '20s, played with the new technology.

It was inevitable that corporate rock, bereft of ideas and running on the '60s, would arrive here too. It was inevitable that it would scoop up from this hotbed of highly person-

alized art, a single sustaining idea. It was inevitable that almost a decade later — and long after Bowie had abandoned techno-pop for big band revival bop — the sound of synthesizers could be heard on country records.

Bowie, anonymous, living out from behind his creatures, created his most personal work here.

A MORE THOUGHTFUL SCENE IN WHICH PETER TOWNSHEND OFFERS AN EXPLANATION — AND THE PLAN UNFOLDS A BIT FURTHER.

David Bowie and his audience have never fully understood each other. At one time, the audience thought he really might have been from Mars. At the same time, he was stunned anyone would believe it. But through it all there was one constant: they were dazzled by each other. They're like new lovers, panting hungrily at the mere thought of each other, but feeling a bit uncomfortable — distanced — when they meet.

Bowie does more than create the distance. He manages it, too. He makes it work for him.

This tour, with its *Time* and *Rolling Stone* cover stories, miles and miles of newsprint, albums, mini-L.P.s, made-for-radio interviews, hit singles, sold-out shows, round-the-world

rolling publicity — this tour with its T-shirts, sweaters, instant Bowie histories, special Bowie nights at video clubs, with its confessions of former mistresses and would-be mistresses, with banned videos and two movies — this tour, with more hoopla, razzamatazz, sis, boom and bah — this tour, *the* tour of 1983, the one that followed The Who's finale and the Stones' renaissance, is probably the grandest, gaudiest public display for one of contemporary culture's most private men.

"Two years ago I told everyone he's going to come out again," Boy George was telling me about the man who's tour was dwarfing his own. It was shortly before Bowie's two vast, physical and calculated shows before a total of some 100,000 people in Toronto. Here, he'd extended cabaret to some outer limit it had never expected to go. He was more physical than I'd remembered seeing him. Like an opera singer, he'd come to realize, it seemed, he'd have to exaggerate for stadium shows like these. Every gesture then was larger than life.

Boy George O'Dowd knew something about exaggeration and it knew where it got you. Culture Club knew good pop when it played it. Boy George knew the risks that had to be taken to make sure your ego survived whole. "He's being himself," he said, looking very open and clever at the same time. "What's he's after now is honesty. He wants it."

For Bowie, it's the year he came back to earth from whatever private orbit he was in — well, he came partway back, that is. It's the year he shrugged off his anonymity, talking about son Zowie, wanting to make a better

world; the year he became just a regular guy, no Ziggy, no Aladdin.

For his audience, this was a luxury, this closing of the distance. And they luxuriated in all of his history. For that's exactly what his show was about — his great hits.

Bowie's ability to create this distance has caused its share of confusion, though. And distress. There is, for instance, the question of Stevie Ray Vaughan, the young guitarist from Texas. His playing on *Let's Dance* gained as many raves as anything else on the album: one gracefully written review in a British music weekly noted that the roots of his playing were in southern gospel music and described one of his solos as a "benediction" for the rest of the piece. This was

playing which had an almost visual impact — the cool blue of his solo lines against the block heat of the horns.

Vaughan was a genuine find, and it was announced that a European tour with his own band was also in the works. But then Vaughan announced he *wouldn't* be on the Serious Moonlight Tour, citing problems with middle-management in the Bowie camp.

There wasn't enough money, Vaughan's management claimed, that was the problem. Besides, Bowie's people wouldn't allow him, Stevie Ray, to talk to the press to publicize his own album, *Texas Flood*. A final blow came when CBS Records, in its tip sheet to its dealers, had to scratch out the "Bowie tour" as one of the album's selling points.

But none of this appeared to matter much to Vaughan himself. What *did* matter was the way Bowie, whom he found so fascinating in rehearsal, suddenly vanished. "Before we met I was worried about what he would expect from me," Vaughan says. His voice sounds the way good leather feels, not worn but worn *in*, rich and deep. "I thought he may want something like Robert Fripp. But that wasn't it. He came in and played some old records, the stuff I used to listen to, too. I thought it worked out fine."

He's quiet for a moment. "But I haven't talked to him since. It's been real strange. I'd phone and leave messages. He'd never return my calls."

Those closer to Bowie — Pete Townshend for one — understand this compulsion for privacy. Townshend doesn't accept it, mind you. But he's come to know it's there. He knows it goes well beyond the built-in barrier required for the show business celebrity.

"We'd be together in New York and he'd give me his number to call," Townshend told

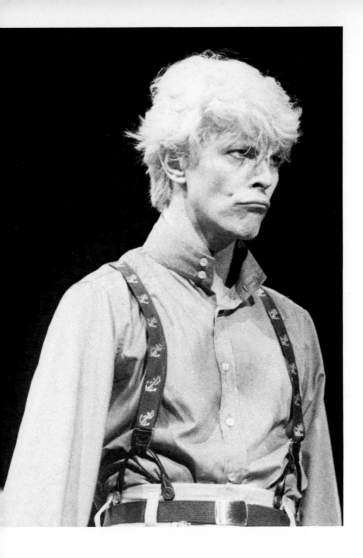

me some time back. "But then I'd call it and it'd be changed. He was always changing his number. He was afraid 'they' would get it. Well, who are 'they'? The press? Wasn't it the press that made him famous in the first place?"

Bowie understands this give-take relationship with the press. Bowie watchers know this, too. "He's got such a tight grip on the media," was Robert Palmer's reaction to the sudden presence of Bowie's image in our midst. Palmer was just beginning his own jaunt across North America: the man with a male model's exceptional looks, but who so far has missed — or escaped — rock's mass marketing image-making process.

The reason I asked Palmer about Bowie — and why a little earlier I'd talked with Bryan Ferry too — had to do with something they knew better than most: something that went beyond the mere marketing of a rock star.

The new supertours — first by the Stones then The Who — resulted in some image-mongering on a vast scale. When the Stones were out you simply couldn't avoid Mick Jagger's face.

Bowie was upping the ante. A lot. He was marketing an attitude — *his* attitude.

But a bit of digression here. Pop's most potent persuader has always been visual: the appearance of the thing. But a distinction must be made between the kinds of images being hustled. All visual styles are arranged self-consciously, but only a few — and Bowie's is very much one of them — have the self-consciousness built right into them. With Bowie (or Ferry, for that matter), it goes from a look to *the* capital-L Look.

elegant, urbane, and reeking of sophistication. Ferry may be sleekest, but Bowie's the first one to market it on a mass scale.

The Look is the key to breaking the music's code. "Rock'n'roll is a visual culture," writes Tony Stewart, introducing his fine book, *Cool Cats: Twenty-Five Years of Rock'N'Roll Style*. "An image, a style, can create more of a reaction, more controversy than the music. The look is just as important as the noise."

Right. You knew the ace rocker in your school by his looks alone (and until recently it was always *his*, not her, looks.) In the '60s he was hipper than everybody. In the '70s he was cooler. He was simply... the ideal.

This brings in Bryan Ferry's theory about Bowie and why, this time out, he's not hiding behind any character. Along with this tour came two new Bowie videos, both filmed in Australia, and two movies, "The Hunger" opposite Catherine Deneuve, and "Merry Christmas, Mr. Lawrence." In the former, he soars through a series of make-up changes taking him from his late thirties through to three hundred years old. In the latter, he's a prisoner of war. "Maybe with all this acting he's been able to satisfy his needs for theater," Ferry suggested. "Now he can be himself on stage."

The digression goes a bit further: unlike the sounds of a particular period, which can be a thousand and one things at once, the Look has been remarkably exact. Everyone, star and fan alike, come to agree quickly on how it's done and what it means.

So there was the Elvis Presley-Gene Vincent-Jerry Lee Lewis style, that great sweep of hair, leather and snarl. Next came its shaggy antithesis with the Beatles: happiness as a warm hippy. Various visual styles have emerged in the '70s-'80s ranging from punk's arch-filthiness to the ragtag color of Boy George and Annabella. But these are ways of looking. They have none of the self-consciousness of The Look.

The Look is something else again. It's

T HE MAN IN DISTRESS — 160,000 WATTS — THE MAN
WITH THE BAMBI EYES — THE TRAVELS
OF OUR HERO.

There are twenty-two tractor-trailers hauling
stuff out of here. Roadies are loading dozens
upon dozens of spotlights, three computers
that run the lighting system, a thousand
bottles of Perrier water, and about two
thousand bottles of beer.

The trucks are hauling about 150 people,
including one hairdresser, one make-up
expert, and one rock'n'roll star who's getting
richer by the moment. There's a
160,000-watt PA system. There's more beer
tucked away somewhere else. And all of this
moves fast, down the road to Frankfurt.

And, of course, I'm too late to follow. So I
dash through the hotel lobby, still the same
timeless beige, past some kids sitting there
waiting for Bowie to pass by and...I *thunk*
into Kidd.

That's R. Lyford Kidd to be exact: well off
in that old WASP-money way that's still
around, a friend from school days, an
absolutely brilliant businessman who, by the
age of twenty-nine, had achieved an M.A. in
Business and had been a vice-president
with an international company. He'd quit
that to form his own little company
specializing in international contracting. He
married the daughter of the owner of a rival
firm in fact. He soon folded *that* company in
with his own.

He's tall, over six-foot-two, portly and with
a florid face. He eats and drinks too much.
He's been, as long as I've known him, rather
unhappy.

I heard his marriage was shaky and
something else as well — that he'd "found
himself." That, as it turned out, wasn't the
case. Two minutes with him showed me it
wasn't himself he'd found. He'd found
rock'n'roll, poor devil. Actually, he'd found
David Bowie.

He was on the tour as well, a sort of aging,
gold-credit-card-carrying camp-follower. His
eyes were incredibly alive with it all. "You
know I never listened to the stuff, you know
that," he blathered on, as I tried to edge out
of the lobby. "But my wife had a couple of
records and I started listening. I believe I
started with Major Tom, the easy stuff. Then

Low, the whole album. I couldn't stop listening to it. As soon as I heard about *this* — he waved his arms as if it were the lobby he was talking about — "I knew I had to be here."

I asked about his wife. He grunted something I couldn't hear. So the wife was gone from the picture. His face was now beet-red.

"How long are you hanging around?" I asked.

"Forever," he said.

"We," says the woman, "are from *Time Magazine*."

She flashed a smile like it was a credit card. The man with the big Bambi eyes shrugged. This is Alan Edwards, in charge of the press for the European segment of the Bowie tour, and right now it would appear he'd rather be handling the D-Day invasion.

We're standing in the lobby of yet another hotel, the Frankfurt Plaza. The media blitz is definitely on.

"That's interesting," Edwards says, "half the people in the hall are from *Time*."

"But we really are," says the woman.

"That's what they all said, too."

The pamphlets being handed out around here describe this as "Bowie Jahr." Typically enough, the pamphlets are fliers hustling Bowie records. Frankfurt, as far back as the 13th century, has been a hot trading center.

Records show that it hosted a major fair every six months which attracted merchants, salesmen and hustlers from across the entire continent. These fairs have lasted through several centuries, and the descendants of that early commerce continue to attend the trade fairs to this day. The Rothchild family started here. Books, cars, jewellery — all are given their time in Frankfurt with its huge convention center spreading westward from the turn-of-the century Festhalle, where Bowie is playing.

Much of the old Frankfurt Am Main was bombed to oblivion by the Allies. Of course, now they're back. Americans have made their own memorial to the war by ringing the city with their airforce bases. You can watch Merv Griffin and the World Series on the armed service TV station.

The new Frankfurt is shining and bright and angular against the sky. It rather suits what Bowie has in mind with this tour. This Serious Moonlight is serious business.

Despite exposure in *Time*, not many Americans troop across the Hamburger Alley — what a wonderful name to meet on the way to hear some rock'n'roll! — and into the Festhalle with its salmon-colored facade and huge glass cupola. For someone accustomed to the great grey concrete wind tunnels used for rock'n'roll concerts in North America, the Festhalle is nicely atmospheric. The cupola overhead allows for everything to bathed in a kind of pale, submarine grey.

Inside, I meet the woman from *Time* again. Apparently the magazine has sent its own troops to cut the tour off at the pass and she's rather miffed. *She's* the one who knows most about Bowie. Someone else is getting the interview. We drink beer to pass the time.

Now this, I think, looking around, is a Bowie crowd. They're older here. More serious. Unlike Brussels, he's all they talk about. They're not here for the current hit but, then again, they have a special, almost personal, connection with him.

It's here where he begins a special kind of home-coming. It wasn't that many years ago he came to Germany and ended up in Berlin trying to purge his system of the abuses of drugs, Los Angeles and notoriety.

And it was in Germany that he came upon a new kind of modern rock'n'roll: the sound

of technology. He now says he regrets some of the excesses in synthesizer-technopop-whatever which came out of this. He feels "some responsibility" because of his power as a taste-maker. But this experiment at that time saved his career.

And maybe Germany saved his life. It cooled him out. He found in Germany "a feeling of social responsibility that is over-powering." And he'll quickly point out to you that there was more to Berlin's than North America's reputation for decadence: "Un-divided Berlin was five times the size of Paris."

He found the new Germany wasn't "the lush decadent thing everyone imagined." So it was here he aimed to part ways with the lush decadent thing he himself had been in the past.

His Festhalle entrance follows almost exactly the ones made in Brussels and the show is paced identically. But the hall and the audience create an impact on the show. For one thing, Bowie is surrounded. Double-decker balconies snake along both sides of the Festhalle and folks hang over them or sit on them or put their feet up *on* them and it all makes the room feel terribly...*physical*.

And if anything the band's better. The Borneo Horns — Lenny Pickett, Stan Harrison and Steve Elson — finally make their section's presence felt. Veteran session players all, it would seem that at first they all felt the need to blend in when exactly the opposite was needed. Bowie's music works best when there are forces present in opposition to each other.

His preference in art is Expressionism (he has commissioned several scripts to be made of the Viennese painter, Egon Schiele): strong colors often clashing, strong eruptions of feeling. His songwriting, always in evolution, nevertheless is consistent in one way: it pits forces one against the other, a lyric against a background, a melody against a rhythm, one phrase against another. To play it any other way would be to miss the richness built into the music.

The song order runs mostly true to the form established in Brussels, and he even sings *Heroes* in English although RCA Germany once released it as *Helden*, Bowie's German rendition.

White Light, White Heat is even more passionate than it was was in Brussels. The entire show has more feeling. The crowd is far more passionate too. And all this heat coming from all sides changes the perspective on things for the critics who'd come to dissect the "new" David Bowie.

"It is, of course, contrived," says one to another back in the hotel lobby.

"But of course it is," says another, "but isn't that his greatness?"

"Yes, but the feeling..." the first grumbled.

"The feeling..." nodded the other.

"In Berlin," I remember him telling me, "I had to learn all over again how to do things for myself. I had to face myself."

It was in Berlin in the late '70s when things caught up to him. He found his attachment to son Zowie growing. He found that his wife Angie's attachment to him was withering.

There he was, on the set of "Just A Gigolo," about to play opposite a deadly pale Marlene Deitrich and an over-abundant Kim Novak, and he hears that his wife in asking for a divorce, has said, "I really want David to suffer."

But he already was suffering in another way. "Gigolo" was his second movie, after "The Man Who Fell To Earth," but he felt he didn't want to be another "rock star who tried his hand at acting." More than that, he was telling reporters he didn't want to be a rock'n'roll celebrity at all. "The rock life has absolutely no interest for me," he'd say. He was using it. It was another palette.

Ironically, in rejecting rock he, along with Brian Eno and Iggy Pop and Kraftwerk's Florian Schneider, others who'd rejected all its enormous, complicated, star-making apparatus as well, came up with a new kind of rock'n'roll.

Two nights in Munich follow one in Frankfurt, then the Serious Moonlight Tour swings over into France for two dates in Lyons. But Bowie eventually comes back into Germany to cities where he feels more at home: Hamburg, where after the shows he and a few friends hit a little downtown club, to sit in a corner and listen to the new music, and finally to Berlin.

"In Berlin," I remember him telling me, "I had to learn all over again how to do things for myself. I had to face myself. Being there was *extremely* important for me. I can't tell you how much."

He arrives in Cannes at just the right time — at least for the thirty-sixth Cannes Film Festival. "The Hunger" is not treated well by critics who view it inside the Grand Palais. But he is news. *The* news. Riot police, called in as *papparrazi*, smack each other around — and anyone else nearby — just to get close.

Two photographers keep wacking each other with their fists, jostling for position.

Wack! Click! Wack-WACK! Click-CLICK!

Thank god, a real star.

The same scene is repeated for the screening of his other movie, "Merry Christmas, Mr. Lawrence." The instant reviews, out on the Croisette, are better. Maybe, just maybe, this Bowie is the real thing as an actor.

WHEREIN OUR HERO FLEES FROM HIS PAST —
OLD RENAULTS — ALBUQUERQUE —
AN ENGLISHMAN ABROAD.

The first time I talked to him he was in misery.

I didn't know it at the time, not being an insider of any sort. Later I would find out almost *no* one knew it, even those around him in Los Angeles and Bel Air, where he lived with his "millions of videos," and his beautiful Chinese rug, and where not to have inside info is not to know anything at all.

The distance again. This time it was a double-distance: he'd created a character who was even more remote than he himself was.

He was trying to put Ziggy Stardust behind him and had come up with the Thin White Duke. "He was an isolationist," was the way he described this ascetic ultra-Aryan. "He had no commitment to any society." He was the total antithesis to Ziggy. No young American, here was the old European brought back to life.

There was something else no one knew at the time — early in 1976 this was — that Bowie's tour across North America was a leave-taking. And that it was a set-up, a warm-up almost, for this tour.

I'm sitting in an American-style hotel that looks out over the renovated Place de Bellecour old-town area of Lyons, ringed with solemn 18th-century buildings and centered on an equestrian statue of Louis XIV. This time I'm ahead of the tour.

Lyons has two obsessions at the moment and both are exiles of sorts: Klaus Barbie, the "Butcher Of Lyons," surrounded by round-the-clock guards in a prison just outside the city, and Bowie. Kids have come in from Clermont Ferrand and Dijon and Aubusson, and up from Orange in their old Renault 5s and Deux Chevaux. The French also love spectacle, and Bowie *is* a spectacle.

As Bowie finished touring in America in that dingy winter of '76, he wasn't about to leave the new world for the old but quite the opposite — he had to get back to Europe to find something new.

That was the tour where billboards showed him wearing a hat — a broad-brimmed continental traveller's sort of hat; something that Yves Montand might wear. The hat cast a shadow over his eyes and a coat dangled over his shoulder. It was before this tour that Bowie had said, "I want to be a Frank Sinatra figure."

This Bowie reminded you of the way the late British theater critic Kenneth Tynan once described Bertold Brecht — as the kind of man you always see in a train terminal, always going to some unknown destination.

Since then he's been in a perpetual exile, from England, from Hollywood, from the record business and from the press.

In a way, what one finds now with Bowie began with that last American tour. Now, no one expects anything in particular from him; back then, they'd dyed their hair to the right red-bronze tint.

They were like mirrors waiting to see his reflection in themselves. It was because he'd look out from the stage and see so many of these reflections that he knew he had to strip away the characters.

"To me, it's all a fantasy," he'd told me, leaning close across the couch. "I'm really a comic indulging in my fantasies of what should be, not about myself."

"To me it's all a fantasy. I'm really a comic indulging in my fantasies of what should be, not about myself."

"To me, music is the paint.
 It's not the picture.
 My music allows me to paint—myself.
 Myself. I become the picture."

We were in Albuquerque, New Mexico, a part of the world that he'd come to like — "The panorama," he said. Even then he felt he needed to get away from those parts of the States he knew too well — those parts which thought it knew him too well and kept coming up behind him on the street whispering "Ziggy?" New Mexico was like another country.

In Albuquerque he looked ghastly. Deliberately ghastly; happily ghastly, perhaps.

His head was a gaunt skull's mask. He cupped a brandy snifter gently in his hands. We were in his hotel room after the show. And it had been an exceptional performance.

He'd been planning to get back to Europe even before this tour had started but was delayed because of the shooting of Nicholas Roeg's film, "The Man Who Fell To Earth." Back then Roeg and Bowie were meant for each other. Roeg, in outlining what might have been Bowie's own thinking told *Image* magazine that "I don't think the personalities of the director or artist should be made public. It destroys every kind of illusion."

So Bowie was in the midst of changing illusions and along the way was laying the groundwork for the current tour. He knew his place in America. "The people here came to see an Englishman," he'd said.

"I'm very conscious of my audience's needs and I'm also very conscious of being a stranger, a pioneer almost, in America. An Englishman in America is someone out-of-

place, something bizarre, almost asymmetrical with everything else."

This was by no means a complaint. Much like his penchant for clash and dissonance in his music, he likes to be out-of-synch with his own surroundings. He's tremendously aware of place. He's tremendously aware of being out-of-place. Distance again.

In the earlier days this led to a kind of theatrical schizophrenia: in America he played the Englishman, in Europe he was from Hollywood. He's still true to form this time. This time he's playing the world so he begins his work shooting videos in Australia — "like a young America" he told people —

equidistant from Europe and Hollywood.

In more ways than not he's been miscast. More often than not he's deliberately miscast himself. At the peak of rock's hero worship he became the anti-hero. "I'm a fan of certain of Bruce Springsteen's songs," he said, "but to me the excitement about Springsteen is the perfect example of a culture trying to find archetypes. Rock audiences today don't enjoy the cliches which, to me, produce the excitement."

He has constantly come up with characters which by their very natures have forced him to flee their inclinations and tendencies and fame. "To me, music is the

paint," he told me that night in New Mexico. "It's not the picture. My music allows me to paint — myself. Myself. I become the picture."

Bowie's sketch of Bowie for the '83 tour is all soft flesh tones and warmth. For the last American tour it was as ghastly as his skull's mask face. It was, as he pointed out, "my deeper response to America than I've had before. I used stark lighting with lots of white because it reminded me of Kerouac's vision of America and William Burroughs."

He'd felt "tied" to America. He'd created the ultimate rock star — this Ziggy Stardust — and America had bought Ziggy, hook, line and haircut. Being Ziggy had given David, as

he said, "a rock star's perspective of the country." It also gave rise to a rock star's need for the spectacular, so he'd created the Diamond Dogs Tour very glittery and with yet another character, Hallowe'en Jack, the ultimate urban city kid "who had to cope with a crumbling environment and who didn't know where to run anymore."

It was all, in his own mind, "very Orwellian." It lost a lot of money and the set was dumped in Los Angeles before the tour was underway. And out of it came an entirely new show, the Young Americans show.

What kind of America was it that had created the crumbling American environment? Who were its people? Young Americans

was to be as much a travelling art event as concert tour. He'd show everyone the sketches he'd made of American life. He'd show where Hallowe'en Jack had come from.

Typically enough, *Young Americans* wasn't about people at all but about place. His sketches were honest to the point that they picked up the essential American city music, rhythm'n'blues. (*Let's Dance* travels over much of the same space. In this context, call it the Young Americans Abroad.)

Young Americans was a music without any specific character to hold it in place. It was an abstract centered around a song about an abstraction — *Fame,* which Bowie was encouraged to write after being with

John Lennon (who played rhythm guitar on the track), written around a phrase dreamed up by Carlos Alomar. It was completed in one night.

There wasn't a logic to the sequence of these two pieces of music as much as a chain of reaction. The deeper that Bowie sank into America the more and more difficult he was finding it to get out. He had only one reaction left and that was abrupt and shocking — the Thin White Duke.

The Bowie tour headed south after Lyons before swinging north. In the middle, it was flown head-long over to the gigantic "Us

Festival" in California. The money was gigantic too, $1.5 million.

The day was steaming when everyone arrived and the smog hung thick and heavy over San Bernadino. That morning the promoter, Apple computer magnate Steve Wozniak, announced that this was it, there wouldn't be a festival the following year, that this little number, a fourteen day blow-out, had cost him $10 million. Before Bowie came The Pretenders, Stevie Nicks, Missing Persons and U-2.

It was clearly Bowie's day.

WHEREIN OUR HERO CONSIDERS THE NEW HUMANISM — MERRY CHRISTMAS, MR. BOWIE — GOSSIP, RUMORS, AND GOSSIP ABOUT RUMORS.

For Bowie, the pre-tour period was a time for straightening out the record. There he was telling *Rolling Stone* magazine that "the biggest mistake I ever made was telling that *Melody Maker* writer I was bisexual. Christ, I was so young then. I was experimenting." But then, as if to keep all this straight talk ever so slightly off-balance, he explained to New York writer Lisa Robsinon that "I put myself through every possible experience I could."

Out of this pre-tour media blitz came a kind of reverse spin on the David Bowie story: that his entire menagerie of weirdo characters, Ziggy and all the rest, the freak-outs and put-ons, don't count and never did; that what we have now is this rather pleasant chap in his mid-30s who, by gosh, is just folks.

He boxes and skis for recreation. He bets on American football games. He feels "satisfied with my own individuality," and that he no longer has to constantly explain to people that "I'm not a part of rock'n'roll... but that I used rock'n'roll."

One need not be particularly perceptive to believe that the role-playing hasn't stopped yet — and that it may never stop — and that the one he's now wrapped about himself may be the most difficult yet: the role of David Bowie.

This part may need as much explaining as earlier ones, but it comes as less of a shock. It can be understood at its face value. It's less threatening than weird old Ziggy.

When he left RCA Records, who recorded him through the expansive, erratic and experimental years during the '70s, EMI sure liked what it saw in the all-new and improved Bowie and signed him for a figure reported to be between $10 and $17.5 million. The company, in a generous mood and spending money on other major but durable artists such as Kenny Rogers, knew that with Bowie it was buying more than a particular talent.

EMI was buying a mystique as well. "The concept of David Bowie has achieved an integrity all its own," noted writer Timothy White. Chris Bohn, a writer for *New Music Express*, said: "For every Bowie phase there's a movement in its wake. Even in his absence, David Bowie is somehow present."

"It started in Berlin really, from LOW onwards. I wanted to get into a more personal kind of songwriting... I was unhappy. There were various things I had to sort out in my own life."

Mick Jagger once suggested that Bowie had left rock for acting, and Bowie admitted he had "let up on his music career." Neither was entirely right. In his five-year "exile" he managed to produce a five-song E.P. based on Brecht's *Baal*; the title song for "Cat People," recorded with master discoist Georgio Moroder; and the hit, *Under Pressure,* recorded with Queen.

Meanwhile, he was on Broadway in 1980 as The Elephant Man. John Corry, in a *New York Times* review said, "It was not unnatural to think he [Bowie] has been cast simply for the use of his name." But, that aside, "he is splendid."

He brought to acting what he brought to rock's theatrics — total commitment. Nagisa Oshima cast him as Jacques Celliers, the Allied prisoner of war in "Merry Christmas, Mr. Lawrence", because he had "immense passion, something that superceded reason."

Bowie himself says he's been going about his acting career the wrong way 'round. He told me: "I'm seeking parts that will enable me to work with directors I think I can learn from. It's my obvious and flaunted ambition to direct. It's my intention to work with Iggy Pop in film, if I ever get a chance. He's one of America's finest young actors — I really believe that. Taking on roles is a lot of fun, but it's not something I feel I'd like to have as a career. I've had a lot of experience in a very short time."

It was passion, he'll tell you, that brought him back to the rock stage — passion and money. During those years when he wasn't actually writing or recording, when he was filming in the Pacific, he was listening to music he discovered in the '60s: Elmore James and Red Prysock. What he found there was the kind of passion he was bringing to his acting but felt was lacking in his music.

"Doing the '78 tour helped a lot because after that I became bored with interpreting songs according to the characters," he tells me. Unlike the earlier conversation, all smoke and mirrors, this is direct, business-like, and to the point.

"It started in Berlin really, from *Low* onwards. I wanted to get into a more personal kind of songwriting rather than rely on the theatrical, the dramatic, and the audio experience. I was unhappy. There were various things I had to sort out in my own life: I had to sort out what I wanted to do. I wasn't planning anything. So, I began sorting out all my functions. It was a redefining period. I'd become too used to the American rock'n'roll life-style. It was in in its own way a period of introspective music. A sort of German seriousness about it which probably had a lot to do with my music that followed."

In Los Angeles, he goes on, he was "close to total collapse. I'd had a few years of problems with drugs and drink and whatever. Very serious problems. Physical problems. And they of course affected my mental state. I was very, very unbalanced at the time."

He was looking for order and balance so he looked up Brian Eno and discovered Berlin. He could start at the beginning again. He was a complete unknown in Berlin. No one there was as obsessed by personality as they were in Los Angeles. On one hand he had to take care of himself; on the other, he found a new freedom in being able to walk down a street and buy his own airplane ticket completely unnoticed.

Another learning experience: his discovery of Berlin led him to discover the importance of environment and there, in an environment of machines, with Brian Eno evolving new systems of music, he came to want to understand the interaction of man and machines — those scary monsters.

"During the Berlin period I went through the best of my highs and the worst of my

lows. From then on I was able to develop a positive outlook for myself and my immediate family.

"I think a humanist era is upon us. I think that it will be part of a new overwhelming wisdom, that because of the pressures on their lives, people are looking at themselves. Yet they're becoming less remote. There's a growing need for self-help. People are looking at themselves living in small groups.

"Yet the melting-pot idea is becoming obsolete. I think 'Merry Christmas, Mr. Lawrence' is terribly successful because it understands that the inner tensions in what's supposed to be a war can backfire and can negate everything else and lead to a respect for the differences between people — and it recognizes that those differences are perfectly legitimate and perfectly logical. People *are* different and are proud of it."

What shocked him in Australia, another environment which had intrigued him ("ah,

the colors of the wheat") was the racism he encountered there. He loved the country itself from the time he was first there in 1978. "I found it a completely different country, completely new — it has all the dynamics of a young country just beginning to incur all that comes with a consumer/industrial society.

"There are incredible things happening there: the people are abounding with enthusiasm. There's very little pretentious- ness and they're good at what they do and they work very hard. Pollution doesn't stifle them. There's nothing jaded about them."

But the racism he found there led him to include an anti-racist subtext in his two *Let's Dance* videos and to really *consider* it: "It's the first time I've dealt with it in my song-writing although it's certainly not unusual for rock songwriters and musicians to attempt this strain of writing. For me, though, it's very new.

"I'm trying to find my feet, trying to find a way of expressing myself in this way. The kind of writing I'm intending to do however will deal with more humanistic subjects than some of the darker areas I've explored in the past.

"Not to negate my own past — and I certainly accept responsibility for all that — there's no reason why I shouldn't change my mind, which is, in fact, what's happened. Now I'm feeling more enthusiastic."

In a curious way, tours tend to take on the characteristics of the countries they're in. In France, during a cool, rainy spring that had farmers worried, Mitterand in political hot water, and strikers out on Paris' streets, it came closer to pure show business than anywhere else. It was an escape.

In Gothenberg, Sweden it coincided with school holidays and people camped out for days in tents and ramshackle huts. It was called "Bowietown."

"Everyone was everywhere, everyone was cruising," said someone who floated on and off the tour. "I mean, it was unbelievable. If you wanted to meet a girl you'd just walk up and down, up and down and eventually you'd meet exactly the one you'd dreamed about."

In Holland the tour ran into some difficulty though — an overdose of media, almost.

The three major Dutch TV networks wanted to cover the shows there because they'd created such a stir — some 200,000 tickets had been sold in a matter of hours, and every interviewer wanted a few words with the man himself.

Interviews were impossible to get everyone was told. But the problems really began when the crews were limited to a brief moment in front of the stage before being shown the way out.

In England, some of the press tried to play up the past ("he denies he was ever gay or ever a transvestite"). Most just grabbed at a hunk of Bowie as he passed by en route to the world:

"MY BIG AFFAIR WITH BOWIE"
"The scene was very kinky. I went along it because I was in love.
"I know David was in love with me."

By the time the tour had reached Milton Keynes Bowl (outside of London) for the final stop of the European segment, everyone seemed to know more than they needed to know about him. Still the reviews were generally good.

But it was a sweaty day, with The Beat also doing a set for too many people in too small a place. It was a rock festival by any other name. The band was ready for North America.

Everyone takes a break after Europe except the American public relations corps who are preparing for the North American chunk of the tour which begins in Canada at the Colisee in Quebec City.

A *Time Magazine* cover is in the works, a key to coming up with more publicity.

For my own break, I head back to my home in France. Waiting there was an urgent message from Kidd.

The number he left turned out to be a hotel on the Riviera. Two hours of calling finally located him in the bar of the next hotel.

"You must come here," he said. "It's terribly important."

It was a great, grand pink pile of a building well back from the sea — grand in that way we'll never see in hotels again, with private alcoves and a private beach and a reading room which had first editions which went back seventy years. The halls were broad and wide and empty: you could see where expensive pieces of furniture had once been.

The hotel was just about to open after renovations had been completed when Kidd had shown up, waving his credit card and convincing the chef to "whip up" some "serious dishes."

They'd gone along with pretty much everything except the stereo he'd wanted for his room. It was about then they started to figure something was wrong.

I *knew* something was terribly *right* the moment I'd seen him. He'd lost weight, a lot of it. A sloppy dresser, he was dressed to the nines. He'd dyed his hair blond.

"My dear chap," he began...

Here was one man's Bowie tour, I thought. I could see how the story might be received back home by his business and family. But Kidd, for the first time I'd known him, maybe for the first time in his life, had been liberated in some private way. He seemed to be actually enjoying himself.

What was urgent was a letter he wanted me to take to his wife. "I'm not coming home for a while," he said. And he didn't trust the mails.

WHEREIN OUR HERO TALKS TO A FRIEND,
CARLOS ALOMAR, AND THE TOUR BEGINS — MODERN
STRATEGY — DAVID BOWIE PRESENTS DAVID BOWIE.

"It was in early March, March '83," says Carlos Alomar, "when I got the phone call."

We're walking up Rue Montagne in Montreal and the Bowie band is feeling good and loose. The boss is confident. The Home Box Office pay-TV network is scouting the two shows at the Montreal Forum. The entire show had been revamped: it's something different to play with.

It's shorter. It hits harder. It's no longer electronic out-door cabaret but rock'n'roll — a rock'n'roll concert, Alomar says, designed for North America.

North American acts have only recently discovered Europe but they've come to discover it in a big way. And this, coupled with British acts which have long toured across the continent, has made the touring business suddenly competitive.

Dire Straits was there, doing the smaller halls. Rush was there too, and Rod Stewart and Supertramp — everybody slogging it out for the same bit of rock'n'roll ticket money. ("It was amazing, really," Supertramp bassist Dougie Thomson, told me a little later. "There were so many shows that not everybody could do well. We did well. And Bowie did well too. In England it was amazing — he sold so many tickets!")

In Europe, it all boiled down to an unofficial contest of sorts. But when the Bowie tour landed in Quebec City there was no contest. In mid-July, word was out at least in the music business that the Bowie tour was *the* tour of the year.

It had out-sold the Stones' shows in Paris and in Edinburgh. The three Madison Square Garden shows in New York had sold out immediately. In Rotterdam, more than 100,000 tickets were bought in two hours and more than 200,000 tickets in two days.

So Alomar and Carmine Rojas and two more of us are tramping up the little rise that takes us to the Ritz Carlton and there, in an alley behind the hotel and leaning against a BMW, are two women, two tall attractive

women, dressed well, elegantly almost, and obviously not loitering. They're smoking a joint.

We slow down.

Coolly, without missing a beat, they both shrug and keep passing the joint back and forth.

"Yes?" says one of the women, daring anyone to say *anything.*

Alomar just laughs and we head for the hotel lobby. Craziness. General craziness. Every so often the business rolls to a halt and anything can happen. "Sometimes this is great."

He wasn't on the recording session for the *Let's Dance* album but he and Bowie had been talking over the years about going out on the road again but nothing was ever definite, and then the call came.

Did he want to organize the band?

"Here was the biggest tour in the world but there was little time left, something like two or three weeks to prepare the charts for the rehearsal," Alomar says. "We had to come up with thirty-five songs. But there was no question that we'd get it together. We had to. The only thing about the show was to make the music work so that David wouldn't have to worry about it.

"It was very complex. It was David Bowie presents David Bowie. Everything was designed on stage to allow the audience to discover what that concept is. It may seem vague at first but it develops as a mini-play with David as the central character. You'll notice how the second act is more visual than the first. We work up to that."

The concierge at the Ritz has a problem. Three kids have been discovered on the seventh floor, the band's floor, and they've got ghetto blasters turned up high. Security is called.

Everyone seems mildly shocked. This is *not* the kind of tour where *that* kind of thing happens.

Nothing, but nothing, fazes Carlos. "What we did have to do is prepare a different kind of show for a different kind of audience over here. To the audiences of Europe, he's always been there. He's a household word to them. For the American audiences, you've got to come at them and tear them up. In America you must reintroduce yourself. In America you must be prepared to please the people."

We meet the rest of the band going out just as we're coming in, and as they tromp through the doors with their kit bags, they remind me more than anything else of a baseball team heading to the stadium.

"No one does a tour like this for the money," Carlos goes on. "It's for the prestige. It's something to put in your resume. It's the top tour in the world right now. That's something.

"As for him" — he nods in some unspecified but upward direction — "he's spent so much of his career preparing for this. I mean, for so much of his career he's seemed to be at the top. Now he is."

Quebec City, for all the richness of its past, is a mean, unhappily modern little city, and despite the summer festival which filled almost every available park space with every kind of music, the Bowie show at the Colisee du Quebec was the first real heat this summer had seen.

Down at the bar St. Angele, in the heart of the old city, Dave the bartender and owner had put on all the Bowie records he could scrounge up for the crowd coming in after the concert. In the Parc du l'Artillerir, scalpers were getting $50 Canadian for $15 tickets from the tourists.

The show was taut, optimistic and displayed a lot of savvy.

In Montreal it took on slightly grander proportions and I began to notice something else: the shows came to reflect the cities they were in the way the tour in a broader sense had come to reflect the countries.

In New York, a New York critic — Carol Cooper in the *Village Voice* — picked up from Bowie's Madison Square Garden performance that he was "like the Great White Hope: like Bobby De Niro playing Rudy Valentino playing Ziggy Stardust. 'Star,' indeed."

Alomar never was exact as to what the spectacle was about. And with reason: it was what Bowie all along had said it was about — the frame for whatever painting he was doing at the time.

Nothing ever came easy for Bowie. And none of the benign aloofness that comes from the zillion-and-one photos of him can completely hide what it's cost him. Indeed, that's one of the stranger aspects of this tour. Both the Stones and The Who were worn down on their's, getting paler and thinner and weirder as time went on. Bowie remains the image of himself, as if fixed forever at this time with that Look, by a sheer act of willpower.

About the Authors

Philip Kamin was born in Toronto on February 20, 1955, and makes this city his home. A graduate of Ryerson Polytechnical Institute, he picked up a camera for the first time in 1978 and went on the Genesis tour. His work met with instant success, and since then his photographs have appeared worldwide in magazines, songbooks, programs, publicity campaigns, books and on album covers and posters. In addition to Genesis, Kamin has worked with: The Rolling Stones, The Who, Peter Gabriel, The Cars, Phil Collins, The Little River Band, Van Halen, Black Sabbath, Rod Stewart, Triumph, Ian Hunter, Teenage Head, Martha And The Muffins, Roxy Music, Ian Dury.

Kamin's first book, co-authored by Peter Goddard, is titled *The Rolling Stones Live* (in the U.S., *The Rolling Stones: The Last Tour*). *The Rolling Stones in Europe,* co-authored with James Karnbach, and *The Who: The Farewell Tour* with Peter Goddard, were published in 1983.

Philip Kamin uses Canon cameras and equipment exclusively: F1 and A1 bodies with motor drive; lenses: 24mm f/2, 35mm f/2, 50mm f/1.4, 85mm f/1.8, 135mm f/2, 200mm f/2.8, and 300mm f/4 Aspherical, and Canon strobe system.

Photo by ALLAN STOKELL

Peter Goddard is the rock and jazz critic for the *Toronto Star.* He has written for a variety of magazines in Canada, the U.S., and France, and recently won a National Newspaper Award for critical writing. Goddard has an M.A. in music and a degree in solo piano performance. He has written several scores for experimental film, including electronic music, and has written and produced for television and radio. Peter, his wife and daughter reside in Toronto, and they spend part of the year on their farm in France.

Goddard's first book was on Frank Sinatra, and he co-authored *The Rolling Stones Live* and *The Who: The Farewell Tour* with photographer Philip Kamin. He is currently working on a novel, and has been commissioned to write a history of popular music.

Photo by PHILIP KAMIN